D0586417

LADYBIRD BOOKS

UK | USA | Canada | Ireland | Australia
India | New Zealand | South Africa

Ladybird Books is part of the Penguin Random House group of companies
whose addresses can be found at global.penguinrandomhouse.com.
www.penguin.co.uk www.puffin.co.uk www.ladybird.com

First published 2016
001

Printed in Italy

A CIP catalogue record for this book is available from the British Library

ISBN: 978-0-241-28670-8

A Ladybird Book of

Colouring

Cinderella

606d – Well-Loved Tales, 1964
Author: Vera Southgate
Illustrator: Eric Winter

A LADYBIRD EASY-READING BOOK
'WELL-LOVED TALES'
Cinderella

Tootles the Taxi and Other Rhymes

413 – Fairy Tales and Rhymes, 1956
Author: Joyce B. Clegg
Illustrator: John Kenney

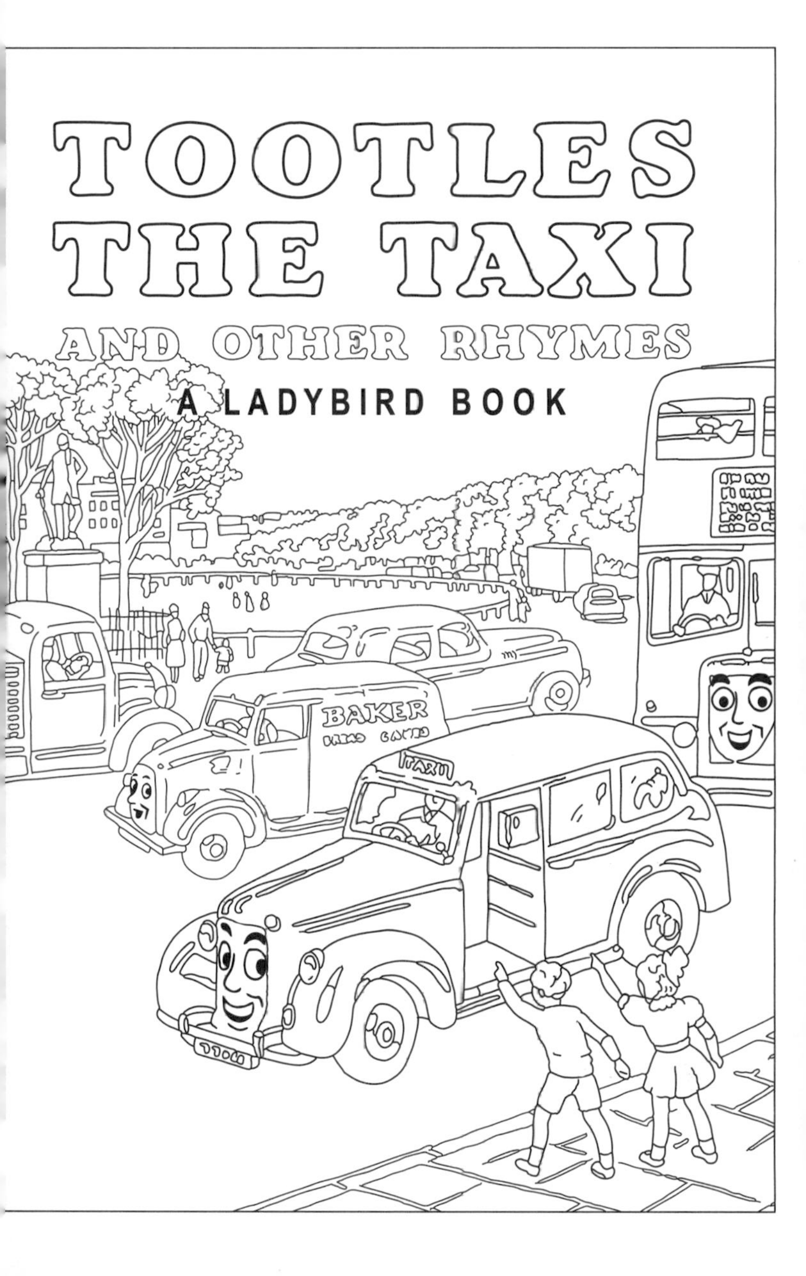
TOOTLES
THE TAXI
AND OTHER RHYMES
A LADYBIRD BOOK
BAKER
TAXI

Learning to Sew

633 – Hobbies and Interests, 1972
Author: Noreen Davis
Illustrator: Eric Winter

A LADYBIRD BOOK
Learning to Sew

The Ladybird Book of London

618 – Capital Cities of the World, 1961
Author: John Lewesdon
Illustrator: John Berry

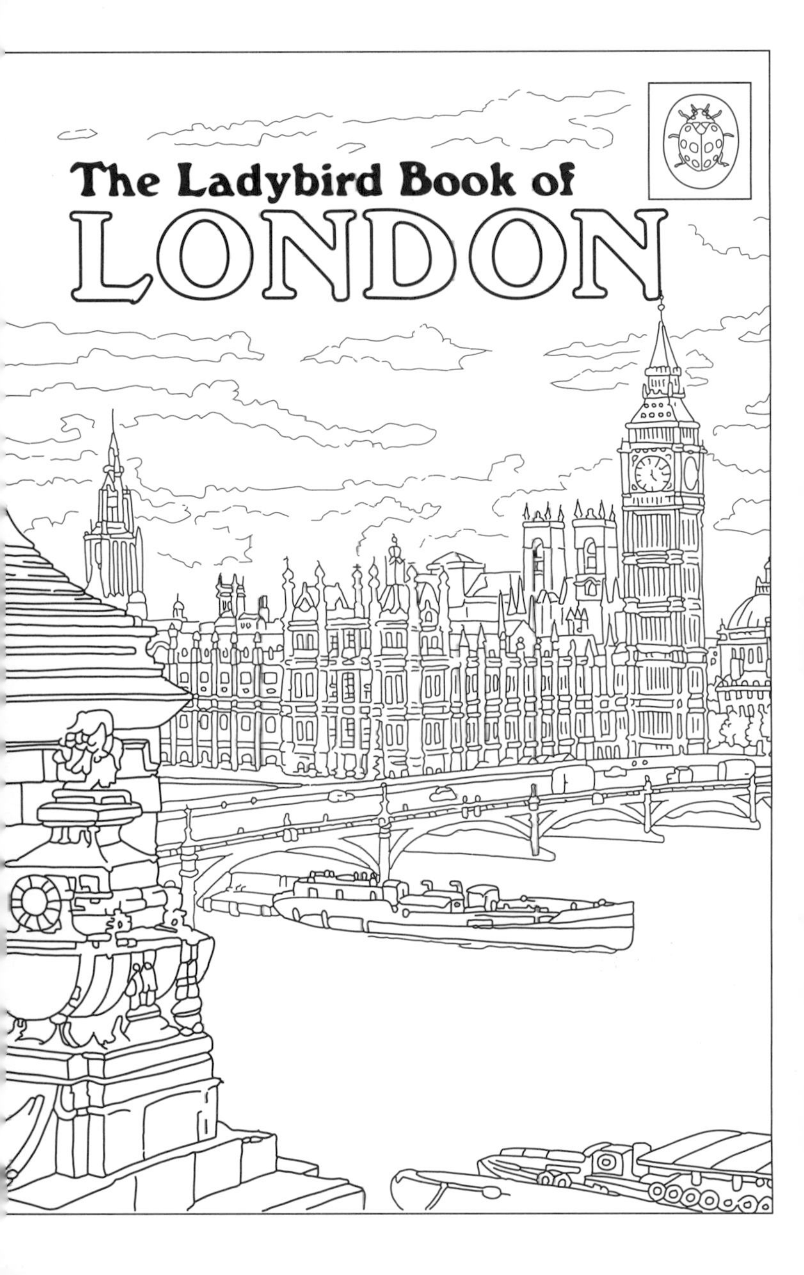
The Ladybird Book of
LONDON

Weather

621 – Junior Science, 1985
Author: Ian A. Morrison

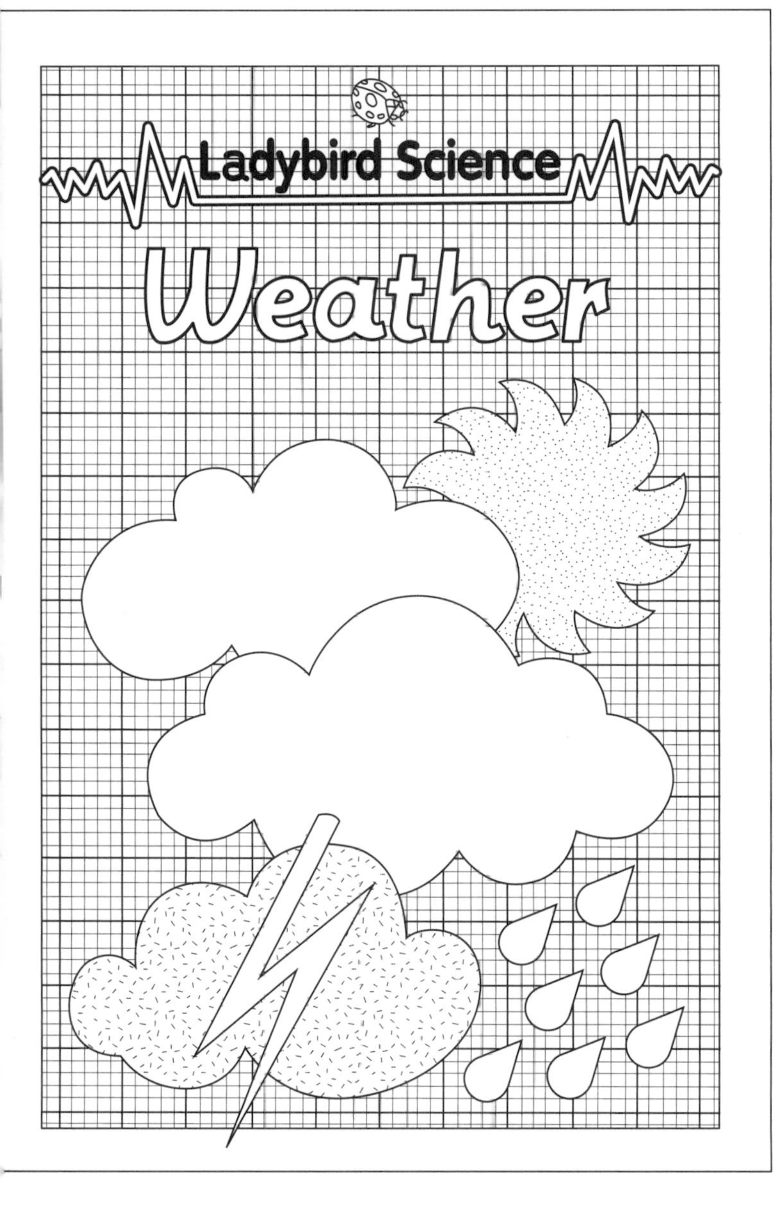
Ladybird Science
Weather

A Ladybird Second Picture Book

704 – Picture Books, 1970
Author: Ethel Wingfield
Illustrator: Harry Wingfield

A LADYBIRD SECOND
Picture Book

Cooking with Mother

702 – Learning with Mother, 1977
Author: Lynne Peebles
Illustrators: John Moyes and Roger Hall

cooking
with
mother
SALT

Flight Three: USA

587 – Travel, 1959
Author: David Scott Daniell
Illustrator: Jack Matthew

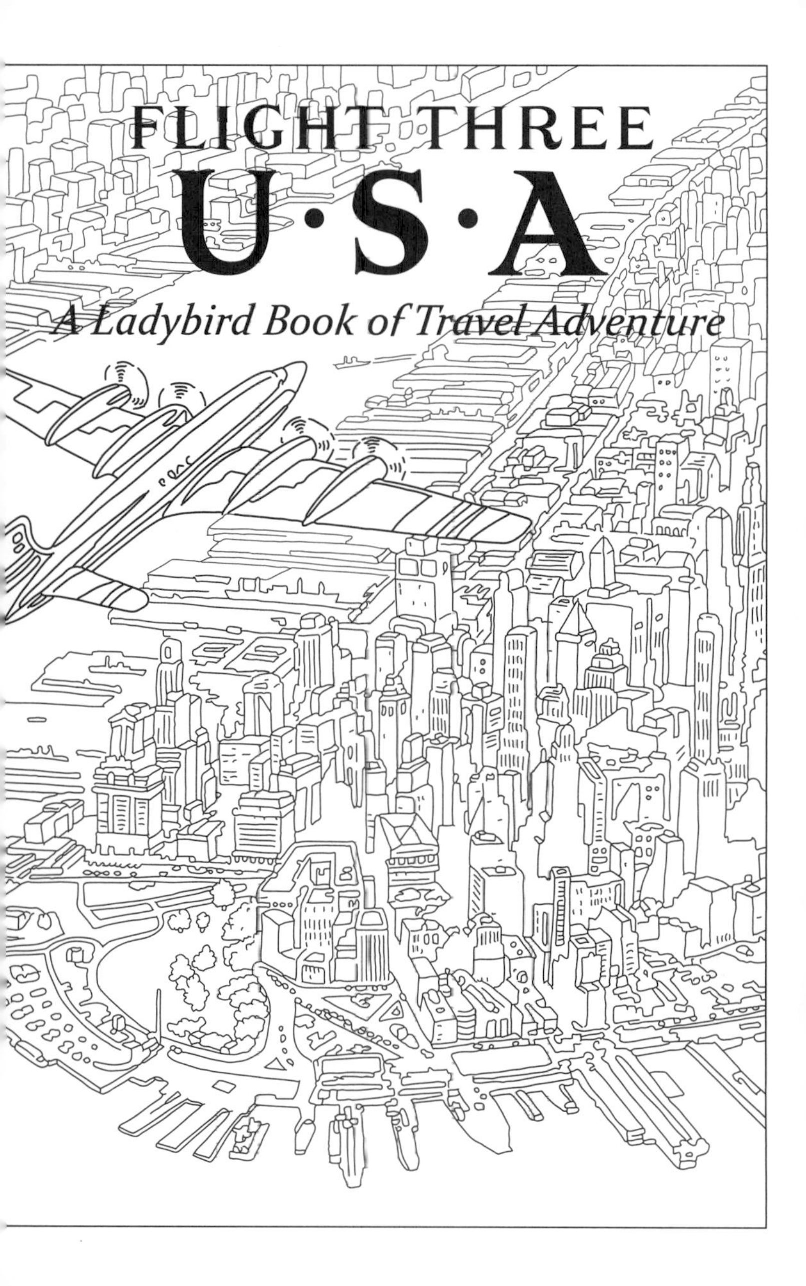
FLIGHT THREE
U·S·A
A Ladybird Book of Travel Adventure

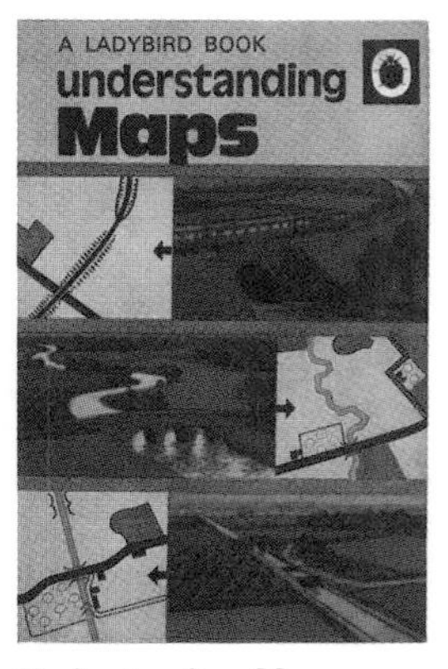

Understanding Maps

671 – Understanding, 1967
Author: N. Scott
Illustrator: Ronald Lampitt

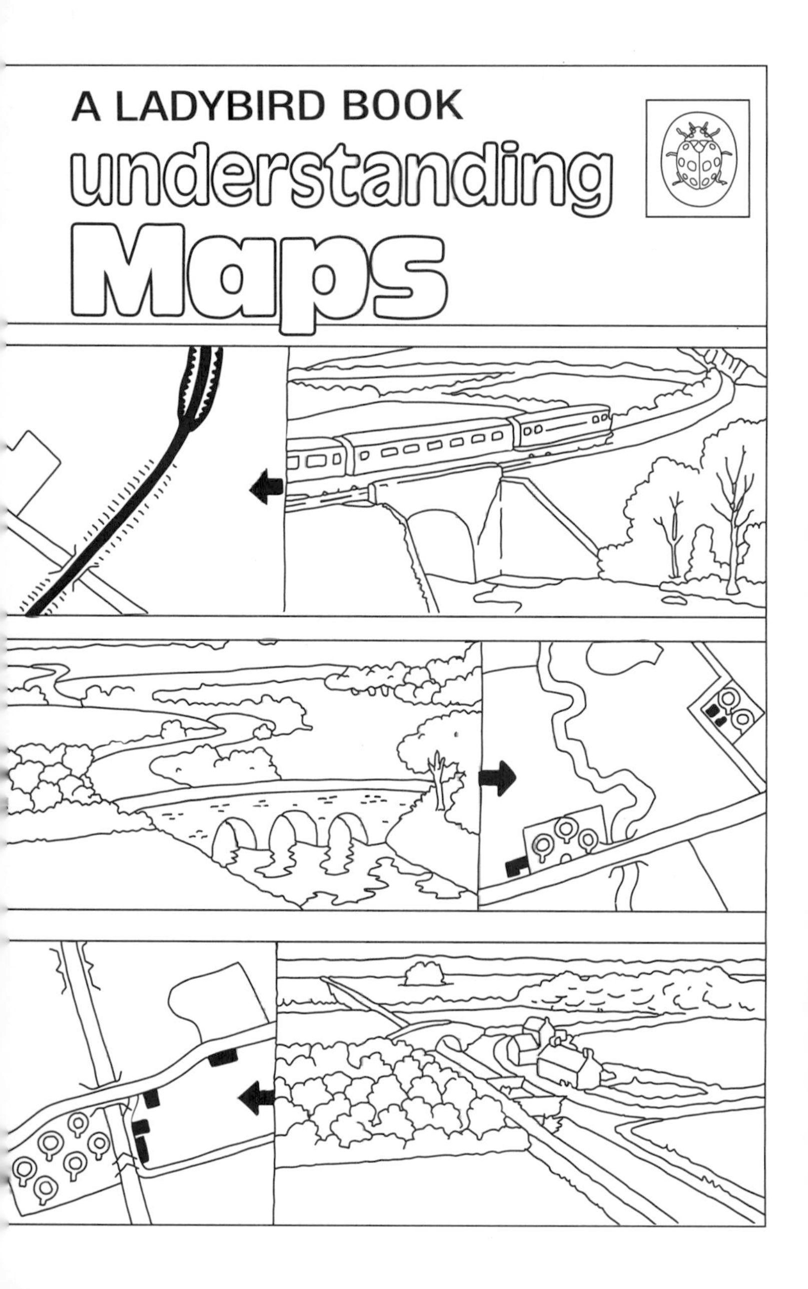
A LADYBIRD BOOK
understanding
Maps

Puss in Boots

606d – Well-Loved Tales, 1967
Author: Vera Southgate
Illustrator: Eric Winter

'WELL-LOVED TALES'
Puss in Boots
A LADYBIRD 'EASY-READING' BOOK

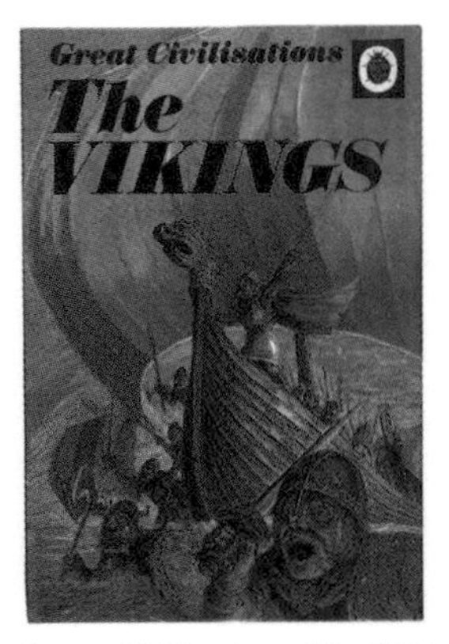

Great Civilisations: The Vikings

561 – Adventures from History, 1976
Author: Brenda Ralph-Lewis
Illustrator: Ronald Jackson

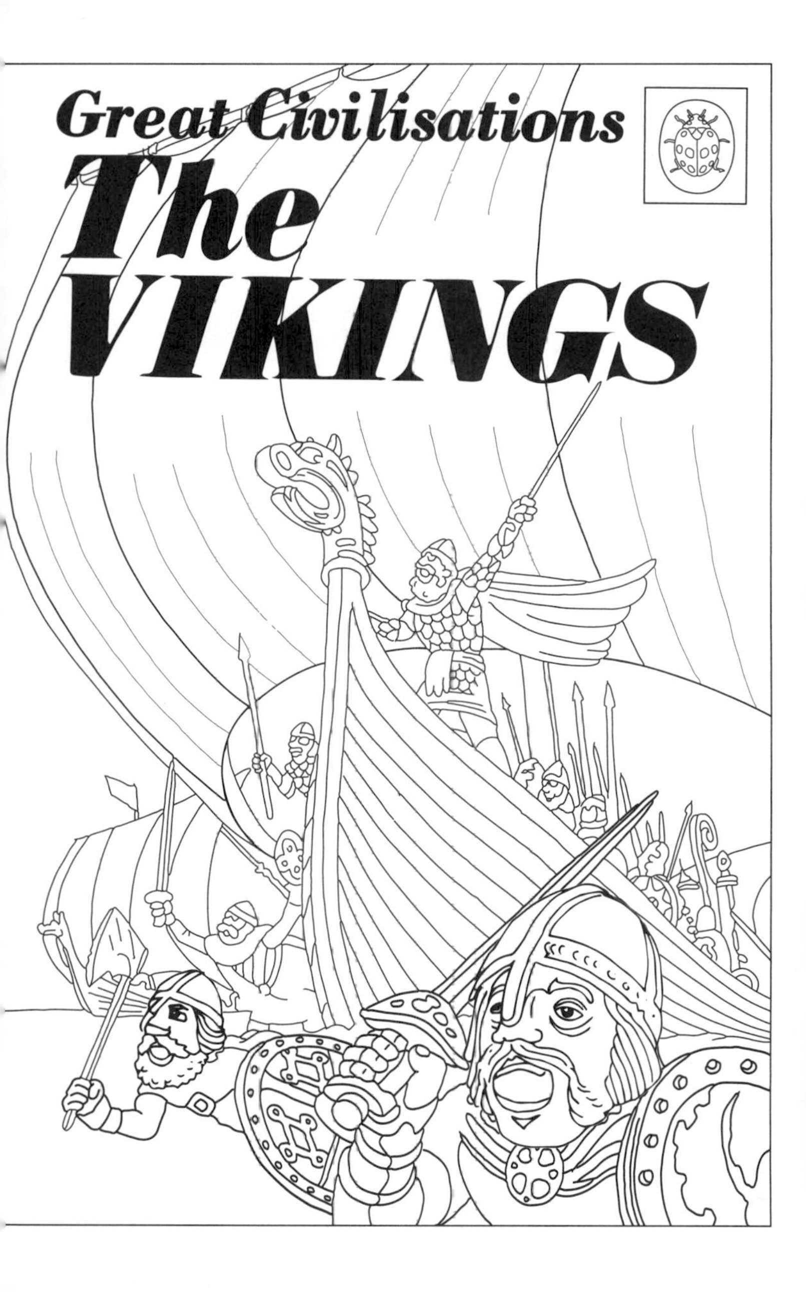
Great Civilisations
The VIKINGS

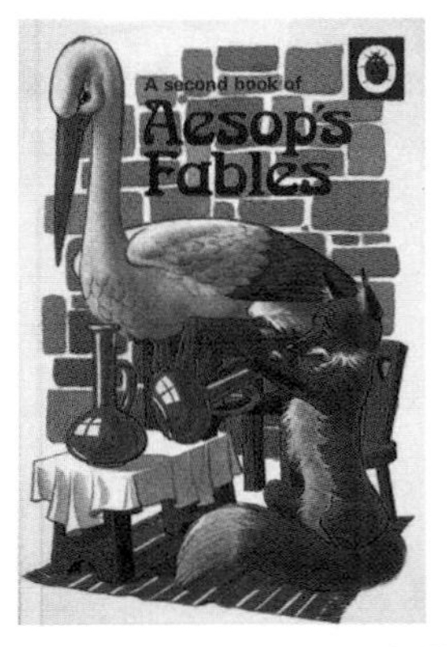

A Second Book of Aesop's Fables

740 – Myths, Fables and Legends, 1974
Author: Marie Stuart
Illustrator: Robert Ayton

A second book of
Aesop's
Fables

A Ladybird Book of Flags

584 – Recognition, 1968
Author: David Carey
Illustrator: J. H. Wingfield

A Ladybird Book of
FLAGS

Learning About Heraldry

633 – Hobbies and Interests, 1974
Author: A. E. Priestly
Illustrator: B. H. Robinson

Learning about
heraldry

The Computer

654 – How It Works, 1971
Author: David Carey
Illustrator: B. H. Robinson

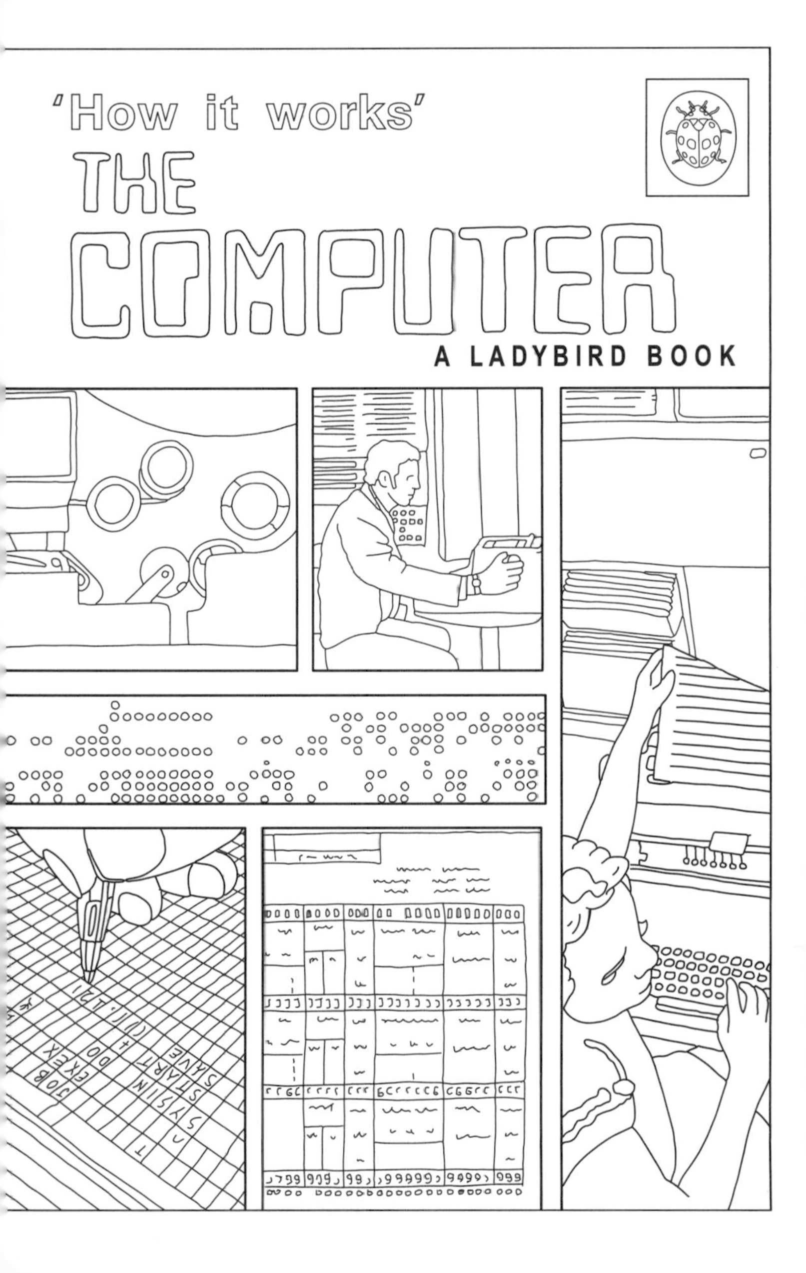
'How it works'
THE COMPUTER
A LADYBIRD BOOK

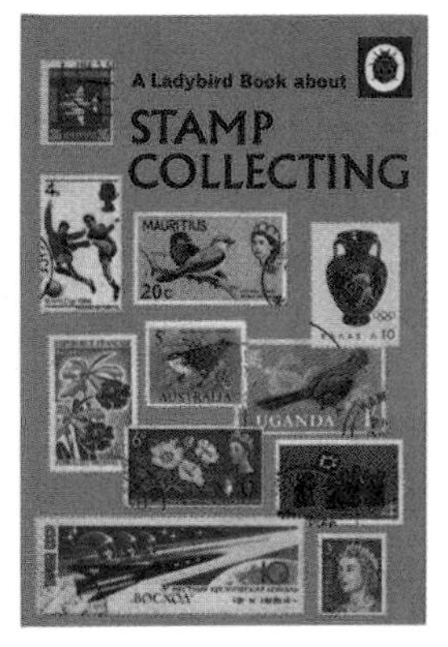

A Ladybird Book About Stamp Collecting

633 – Hobbies and Interests, 1969
Author: Ian F. Finlay

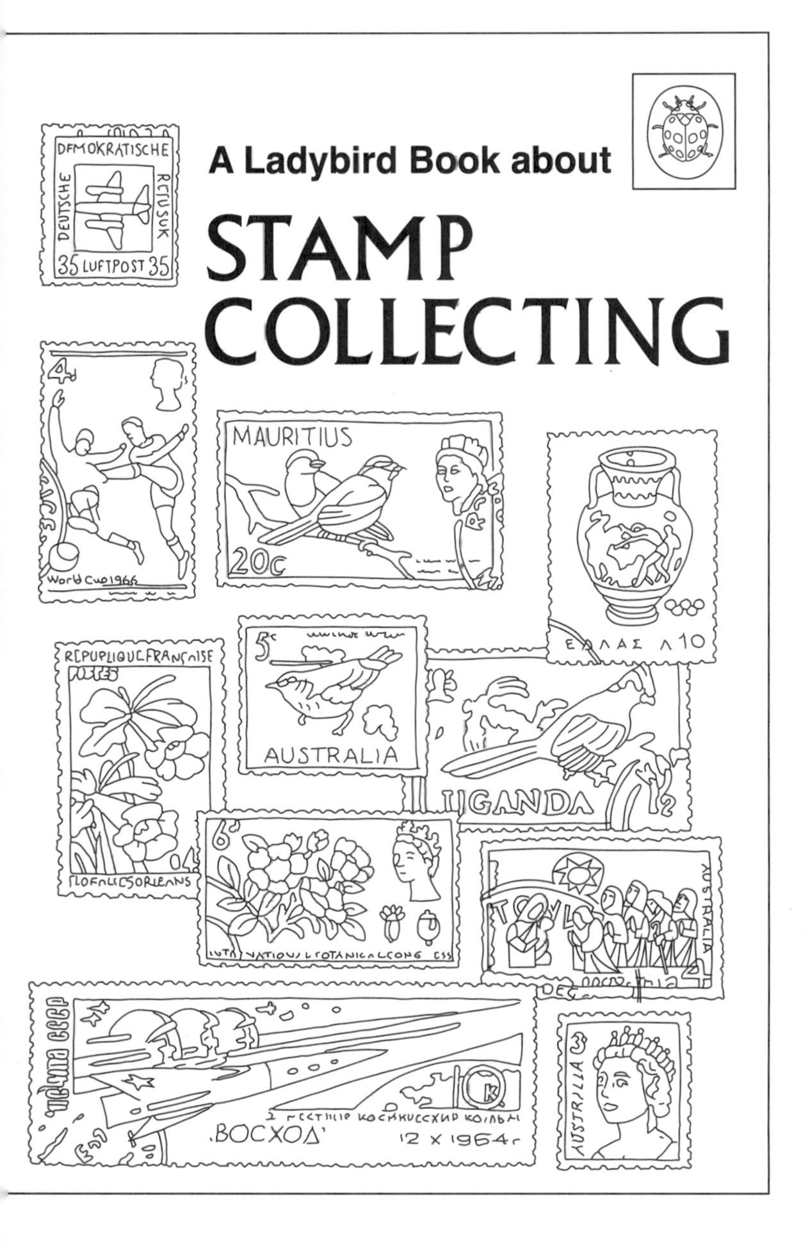
A Ladybird Book about
STAMP
COLLECTING
LUFTPOST
MAURITIUS
20c
AUSTRALIA
UGANDA
ВОСХОД
12 X 1964 г

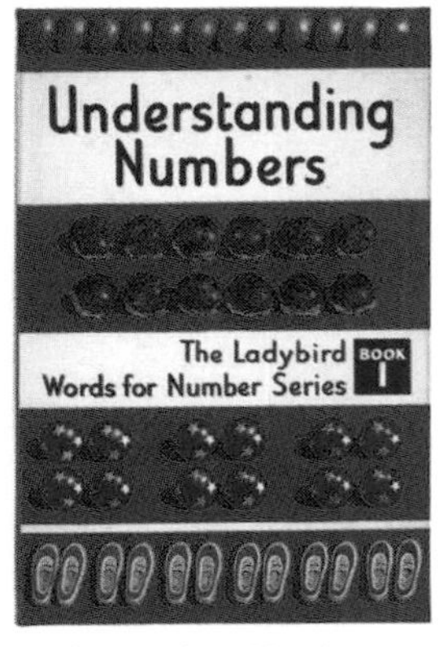

Understanding Numbers

661 – Words and Numbers, 1966
Authors: J. McNally and W. Murray
Illustrator: Kenneth Inns

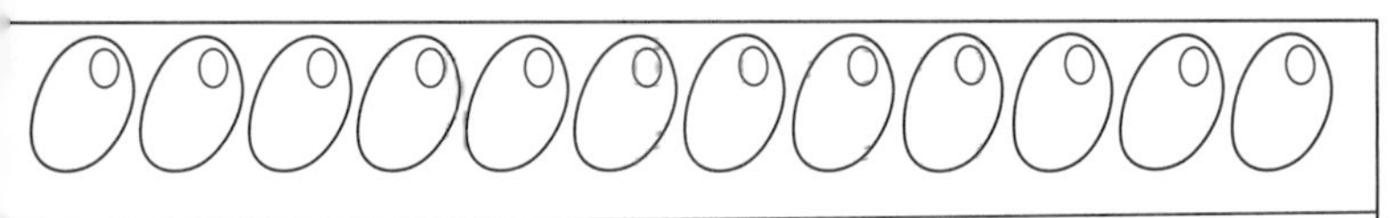

Understanding Numbers

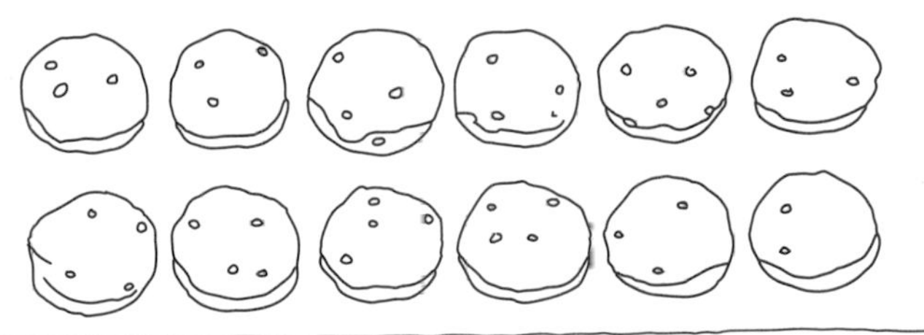

The Ladybird
Words for Number Series

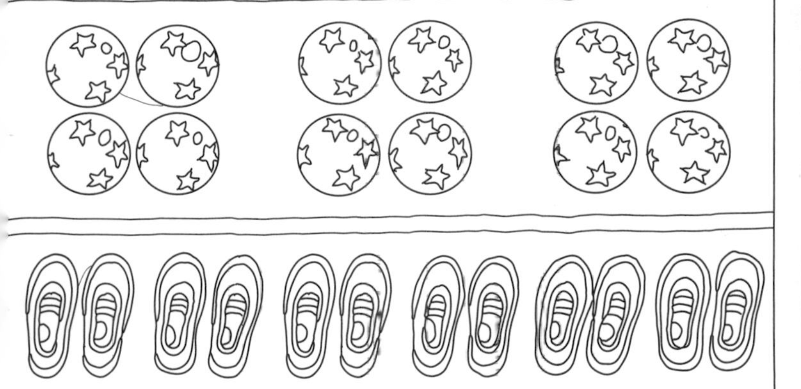

Shopping with Mother

563 – Learning to Read, 1958
Author: M. E. Gagg
Illustrator: J. H. Wingfield

A LADYBIRD LEARNING TO READ BOOK
SHOPPING WITH MOTHER
TEXT BY M.E. GAGG N.F.U.

Things We Do 4a

641 – Key Words, 1964
Author: William Murray
Illustrator: Harry Wingfield

4a
Things we do
The Ladybird Key Words Reading Scheme

The Ladybird Book of Motor Cars

584 – Recognition, 1960
Author: David Carey
Illustrator: David Carey

THE LADYBIRD BOOK OF
MOTOR CARS

Great Civilisations: The Aztecs

561 – Adventures from History, 1978
Author: Brenda Ralph-Lewis
Illustrator: Robert Ayton

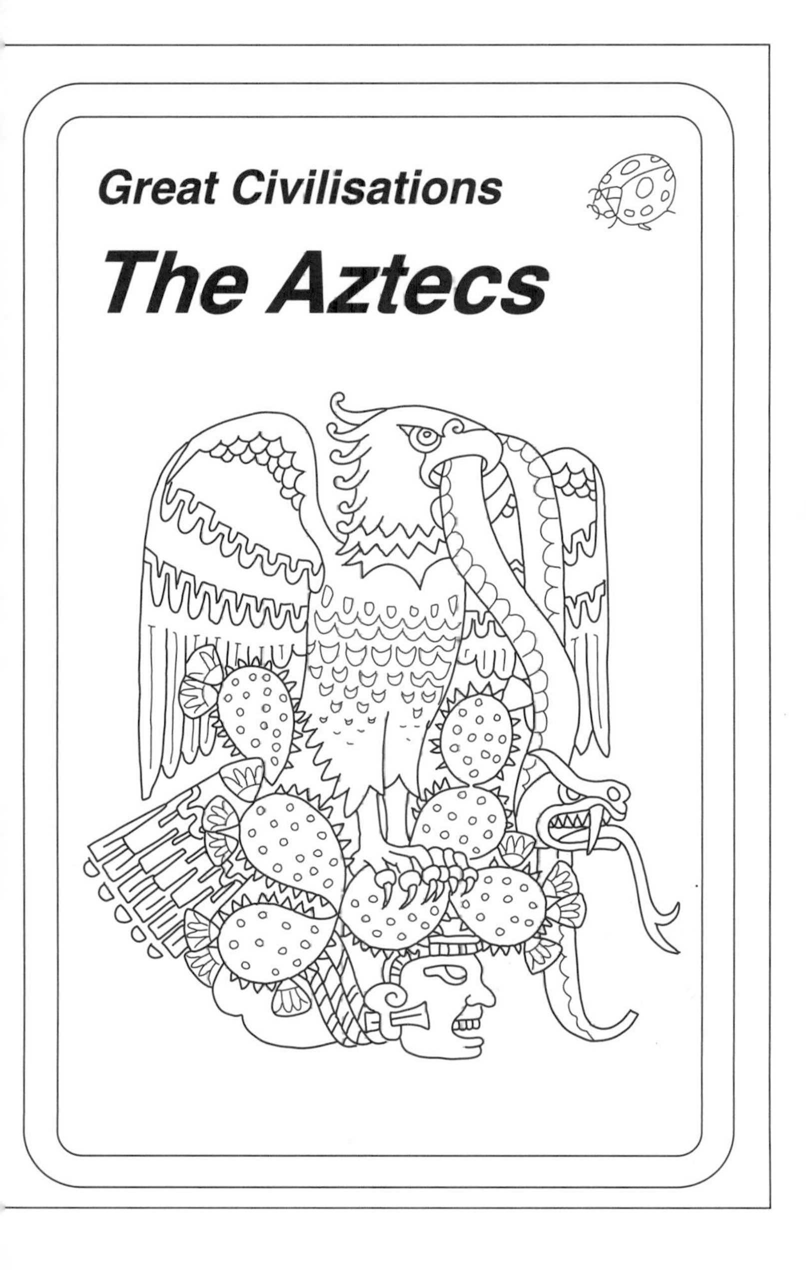
Great Civilisations
The Aztecs

On the Move

833 – Toddler Books, 1983
Author: Lynne Bradbury
Illustrator: Ken McKie

Ladybird
Toddler Books
on
the move

Easy-to-make Puppets

633 – Hobbies and Interests, 1973
Authors: Ian and Brenda Stockwell
Illustrator: Eric Winter

Easy-to-make
PUPPETS

Play with Us 1a

641 – Key Words, 1964
Author: William Murray
Illustrator: J. H. Wingfield

1a
Play with us
The Ladybird
Key Words Reading Scheme